Exposing Bitcoin in Pictures

Bob Seeman

CyberCurb

Copyright © 2021 Bob Seeman

All rights reserved

No part of this book may be reproduced, or stored in a retrieval system, or transmitted in any form or by any means, electronic, mechanical, photocopying, recording, or otherwise, without express written permission of the publisher.

ISBN: 9798451535875

Cover design by: CyberCurb

For Nicola, my personal professional photographer

"A picture is worth a thousand words."

– Derived from Henrik Ibsen

With great ignorance comes great confidence.

As your financial adviser, my advice is that this year we are very bullish on "even".

7

GoFind

How to treat gambling addiction|

Search

I'm feelin' lucky

I had a great time with Daddy at the zoo.
One of the animals paid 40 to 1.

Find out how dumb you are

This is my virtual holiday that I purchased with my virtual currency.

Gamblers Anonymous
Meetings all day and night

Our gambling addiction hotline would do way better if every 10th caller was a winner.

I was addicted to the hokey pokey... but turned myself around.

Please gamble your life away responsibly

15

They say trading bitcoin is addictive and destructive but it brought our family closer. We now all live in one room.

I have learned that, if I am the first in and first out, Ponzi schemes are an excellent investment.

I will give you a big bonus in bitcoin if you can explain to me what it is.

My wife thinks I care more about bitcoin than our kids.
To prove it's false, I will keep trading until I win our son's tuition back.

Don't let the white coat fool you. I don't know what the hell bitcoin is.

You wouldn't happen to have some food instead?

You ask, "Bob, how do I become filthy rich?" It's easy. By scamming others as I am about to scam you.

Class: The beauty of bitcoin is that we can all become rich if we keep buying it.

They say one in every six friends has a gambling addiction.
My money's on Fred.

Which cryptocurrency bubble have you invested in?

Four "Money for Dumbdumbs" at $14.95 each.
That's $189.95.

I made $20,000 mining bitcoin.
After electricity costs, that's a profit of $2.06.

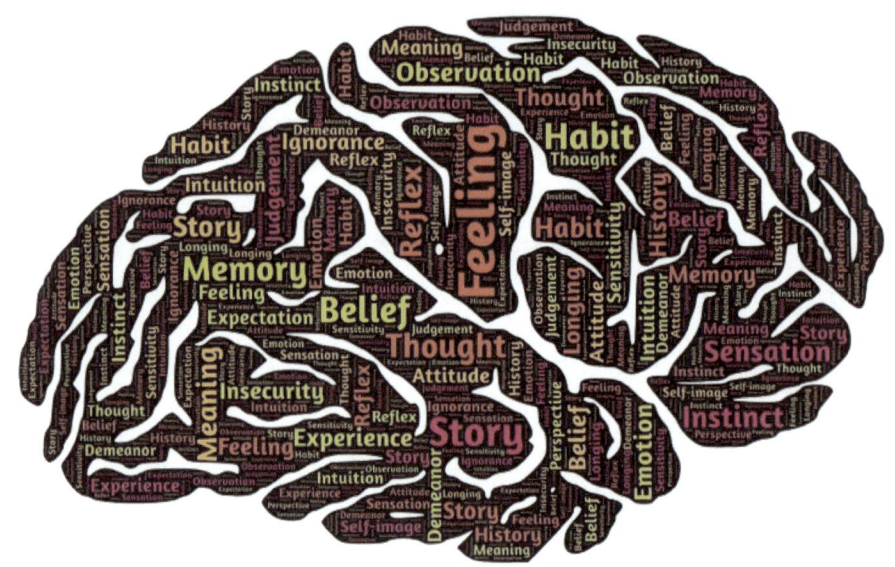

www.ingramcontent.com/pod-product-compliance
Lightning Source LLC
Chambersburg PA
CBHW041945240526
45473CB00033B/601